The Power of

I AM

and the Law of Attraction

The Power of
"I AM"

and the

Law of Attraction

By R.J. Banks

www.RobertJBanks.com

For information address: Crystal City Publishing, LLC.,
P.O. Box 64-1181, Los Angeles, CA 90064

R.J. Banks
The Power of I AM and the Law of Attraction
Printed in the United States of America

ISBN: 978-0-9916231-0-5 (Paperback)
ISBN: 978-0-9916231-1-2 (Hardcover)
ISBN: 978-0-9892485-9-4 (eBook)
ISBN: 978-0-9916231-2-9 (Journal)

Publisher – Crystal City Publishing, LLC.

Cover Design – Cre8tive Minds and Avanzado

Editing – Eric and Crystal City Editing Team

Crystal City Publishing, LLC
www.crystalcitypublishing.com

R.J. Banks 2014. All Rights Reserved

ACKNOWLEDGMENTS

"When I was a child, my Mum would always tell me that happiness was the key to life, it was all you needed. When I went on to school, my instructor handed out paper and asked us to write down what we wanted to be when we grew up. I wrote down "happy". They told me I didn't understand the question. I told them they didn't understand life- *Anonymous (an unverified quote by John Lennon)*

A special thank you to Linda Perry and Christina Aguilera for blessing us with the song (I Am) Beautiful

TABLE OF CONTENTS

DEDICATION

This book is dedicated to all who shall be inspired by reading it.

Introduction

Whether you know it or not, or like it or not, every day you are reciting affirmations to your mind to program your inner self, or subconscious beliefs about you and your life.

Positive affirmations such as *"I am great"*, *"I am healthy"*, *"I am wealthy"* can work wonders for your life. Unfortunately, negative affirmations such as: *"I am so tired"*, *"I am so fat"*, *"I am so broke"*, *"I am so stupid"* also have a very effective power in our lives.

It is the Universal Law of Attraction at work. It has been proven time and time again that:

> *we are, and attract into our lives, what we think, say and believe about ourselves and our perceived reality.*

I'm sure you've felt like you were going crazy at one time or another because things just weren't or aren't working out the way you want them to. I know it's very frustrating but, the question to ask is what have you been telling yourself? Read the first paragraph again. Chances are, you've been wanting something different than the above statements, yet these are the results for the things you have programmed your lives with.

You keep trying with no success or you simply don't try at all. Either way, life keeps going and your situations remain the same. Does any of this sound like what's going on in your life? Well here and now is where you can make the change! You make the change to be positive. The change to a happier, healthier and wealthier life.

Albert Einstein defined Insanity as:

"Doing the same thing over and over again and expecting different results."

He also claimed
"We cannot solve our problems with the same level of thinking we used when we created them."

Yet, how many people do you know, including yourself, who have ever taken a class on how to improve their THINKING? I don't think there are any schools out there that even offer a course like that. I'm glad you found this book as it can serve as your self-study course in creative and developmental thinking, a.k.a. positive Psychology 101.

By changing your thoughts, words and beliefs, you will reprogram your subconscious mind, thus changing your life and what you attract into it. It really is that simple, but for some, it's easier said than done. This book will help you understand how The I AM power can and will work in your life.

I have found that the first person "I AM" affirmations have proven to be the most effective method of reprogramming one's subconscious mind and attracting positive results into one's life. This has been proven over and over and over. It is a Divine Universal law.

The very first thing you need to do to set change into motion is to decide to be positive. You must be very focused on staying positive, no matter what the situation. This, as I just stated, is the very first thing you need to do. I know for many, this is where the first "yeah right" pops up. I understand and I know it may be challenging to fully grasp this concept right away. However, please have an inner discussion with your ego and tell it you are going to stay open minded while reading and studying this book. Training your mind to think and stay positive does require discipline and practice, but the results are phenomenal. Remember, everything that starts in the physical realm as a thought that turned into an idea that turned into words that turned into a manifested miracle in the physical realm.

In this book, I share with you what has proven to work for me. I have been studying this amazing life guiding and creating concept most of my life. Starting in childhood and moving into adulthood, I have read countless books on the subject as well as tried, practiced, implemented and incorporated several "techniques" or "beliefs" in the attempt to create the life I desire. Through many trial and error adventures, what you find in this book is what I have discovered to be effective in my life. My desire is that by sharing what I have learned, you as well will learn how to create the life you desire.

Although this book seems shorter than other books you may find on the subject, my reading and learning styles have rolled over into my writing style as well. This book is more pragmatic than idealistic or philosophical. In other words, no fluff or blah blah blah stories that go on and on in order to "fill" the pages. When I was in the radio/music business, we had a saying directed to the performers: "Don't bore us, get to the chorus." Well, this book is my chorus.

The areas of study I focus on are Scientific, Psychological, Philosophical, and Theological. I understand and respect that there are many different beliefs within each of these disciplines and as I stated. I am sharing what works for me. I was raised in a Baptist/Presbyterian setting; therefore, my theological references refer to the Bible, as this is what I was taught. I feel that most everyone agrees and believes that we are all created by and from a higher source: God, Yahweh, Elohim, Allah, Jehovah. There are several names for our higher source, and whether you agree or believe in this concept or not, it will not affect the results you will get from this book. The scientific references are based on neurobiology and neuroaxiology. The Psychological references are based on the teachings of Positive Psychology i.e. rather than focusing on "mental disorders". The study of Positive Psychology is primarily concerned with using the psychological theory, research and intervention techniques to understand the positive, adaptive, creative and emotionally fulfilling aspects of human behavior.

Before we get into the nuts and bolts of this book, I ask that you please get your I AM Power Companion Journal to write in. You may also get a pre-divided notebook or even use individual composition notebooks. Grab a pen, and a yellow highlighter and make sure you have these items with you whenever you read. If you don't have your journal, label your notebooks with these titles:

1. General notes and written exercises
2. Gratitude Journal
3. Desires Journal
4. Affirmations Journal
5. I AM four forty journal

Later you may also want to get one or more poster boards, at least 22 x 28, a glue stick and scissors.

I am affirming that all who read this book and apply my suggestions be blessed with an ever fulfilling happy, healthy and wealthy life.

The Power
of the
"I AM"

CHAPTER 1

The Power of the
"I AM"

There is a power in our words, that is, in my opinion, truly inexpressible. There is a power so strong, so forceful that it can and literally has transformed entire civilizations and altered the course of history. ***"Mightier than the sword,"*** this power comes from our words. It comes from what we say about ourselves and the world around us.

"I AM..."

These two small words possess the most incredible, life-altering power than all others. The words "I AM" are yours and yours alone. No one else can say "I AM" for you. Only YOU can make the "I AM" statement for yourself. Pastor Joel Osteen declares "God created our words to have creative power. What follows the two simple words "I AM", will determine what type of life you have and will either bring success or failure in your life.

As Dr. Wayne Dyer explains, you are capable of creating anything you desire in your life. Every time you use the words "I AM," you're quoting the name of God, and this is your highest self.

As a biblical reference, when God appeared to Moses in the burning bush, Moses asked,

> "Who exactly am I supposed to say sent me?"

God answered,

> "I AM. You tell the children of Israel that 'I AM' sent you to them. This is my name forever, the name you shall call me from generation to generation." (Exodus 3:11-15).

In the New Testament, Jesus states,

"I AM the Way, the Truth, and the Life."

Truly, "I AM" is the Way. "I AM" is God. He also states that it is not "him", Jesus the man, that is speaking, but rather God speaking through him when he says "I AM."

The power of "I AM" unifies each of us with the power of God (Matthew 19:26).

"I AM" means that I am one with the creative power of God. I am one with the creative power of Life. I am one with the creative power of the Universe.

When you say "I AM" and concentrate on positive things, you create positive experiences in your life.

"I AM" safe. "I AM" healthy.

"I AM" prosperous. "I AM" loved.

Unfortunately, fear and pain keep many of us focused on negativity. If you believe you are sick, unworthy, or destined to fail, then you are. In light of this fact, Henry Ford's famous quote,

"Whether you think you can or you think you can't, you're absolutely right," really rings true here.

On a scientific and neurobiological level, with a twist of psychology thrown in, one can actually become addicted to negativity, e.g., "The Drama Queen". When we think of addiction, we often think of substance abuse with outside sources such as alcohol and drugs. However, addiction actually comes from our own biochemistry being stimulated by these outside sources.

Emotions are also a chemical response to an outside source. We are constantly having emotional responses to whatever happens in our environment. There are receptors throughout our bodies for all the different emotions we experience. There are also neuropeptides, or chemicals produced by your brain, for each emotion.

In a situation when your environment causes your brain to secrete the neuropeptides for fear, anger, jealousy, or sadness, for example, they make their way through the blood stream and lock into the receptors. This causes all the physical manifestations of the given emotion to arise. As the emotion subsides, these neuropeptides are released from the receptors and eliminated from the body. Notably, these receptors are the same ones that accept outside chemicals like drugs and alcohol.

Now, just as with drug addiction, the more these receptors are used, the less effective they become. The body then produces more of a particular kind of receptors to compensate for the loss and damage. More neuropeptides must be produced for the new receptors and thereby creates an overabundance of emotional receptors, which are all looking for neuropeptides. Thus, "emotional addiction" begins.

Emotions give you feedback on how things are going for you. To change an addiction to emotions, you must first understand that you own them. You are 100% responsible for how you feel. No one can make you feel good or bad without your permission. Remember, emotions are good; however, out-of-control emotions are NOT.

So, how can you look beyond present fears, negativity and pain to create positive results in your life? You have to change your way of thinking and realize that you control your emotions, and no longer allow them to control you.

By starting positive "I AM" affirmations, you will begin to reprogram your core inner beliefs. Affirmations are short, clear statements of your desired goal. They are designed to make positive changes in your conscious and subconscious mind.

By articulating the thing you wish to manifest, without worrying about how you can or will accomplish it, you enable divine intervention and universal powers to begin co-creating with you.

Your "I AM" affirmations must be completely positive, with no negative words or ideas (e.g., no, not, stop, refrain). They must also be in the present tense:

"I AM strong."

If you affirm in the future tense,

"I will be strong."

This keeps the strength you desire somewhere far in the future instead of bringing it into your present being.

Those of you who've read *The Prayer of Jabez* by Bruce Wilkinson may recognize, this prayer is very much an affirmation:

> *"Oh, that you would bless me indeed, and enlarge my territory, that your hand would be with me and keep me from evil that I may not cause pain"*

(I Chronicles 4:9-10).

The power of that prayer is truly released when one sees what it is affirming.

1. I AM blessed indeed.
2. I AM growing and prospering.
3. I AM guided and protected by the hand of God.
4. I AM a blessing to others.

The power of the "I AM" is what you declare through your "I AM" statements. It attracts and initiates an incredible creative process, thereby producing every condition, event and circumstance in your life just as you declare and believe it will, without fail and with unfaltering certainty.

Simply put, you cannot speak in negative terms about your life, yourself, or your future and expect positive results. An abundant life cannot manifest when you speak of your life as being filled with deficiency, lack, shortage or bad luck. Remember,

> *"We are, and attract into our lives, what we think, say and believe about ourselves and our perceived reality."*

I cannot emphasize this enough. *We are, and attract into our lives, what we think, say and believe about ourselves and our perceived reality.*

Similar to the law of attraction, many people do not realize the incredible power of the 'I AM" statement. Without thinking about what they're saying or affirming, they constantly create very negative 'I AM" affirmations. They go through their day saying things such as "I AM so tired", "I AM so stupid", or "I AM so fat and ugly". However, when you declare these statements you are affirming that this is your reality, and you will most certainly feel tired, dumb and fat-and-ugly. Or, you can choose to go through your day proudly and strongly declaring 'I AM energized", "I AM smart", "I AM so good-looking!" The choice to set and maintain the tone for your day and your life is in your own "I AM"s.

The power of the "I AM" is simply understanding and learning how to create your desired life by using the law of attraction in <u>your</u> favor and combining it with positive "I AM" affirmations. These two universal and divine powers are always at work in our lives, whether we are cognizant of them or not, so let's use them to our favor!

The Scriptures says, *"We will eat the fruit of our words."* In other words, the realities are produced by what we say.

Joel Osteen suggests that you have to send your words out in the direction that you want your life to go. If you want to know what you will be like five years from now, just listen to what you are saying about yourself today. With our words, we can either bless or curse our future.

The power you possess with your "I AM" is truly the key, or shall I say the 'password', to unlocking, accessing and manifesting your desires.

The Universal Law of Attraction

CHAPTER 2

The Universal Law of Attraction

When we were young, we were very impressionable and believed just about everything we saw and were told. We also spent a lot of time using our imagination, which seemed capable of making anything possible.

For me, it was a most fascinating time. I had such a vivid and wild imagination that I would often get lost in another world or dimension going on some sort of adventure for what could and often would turn into hours. This was great on the weekends and after school but not so productive during class, at least from my teacher's perspective.

As we grew older and were taught a few lessons from the school of hard knocks, many of us stopped accessing our imagination and developed an "I'll believe it, when I see it" attitude. In school, we learned about our wonderful and fascinating universe through science classes. For many of us, this was our first opportunity for a "hands-on" approach performing experiments in the science lab. We also learned that the findings from our experiments were established by using one or more of our five senses. If we cannot see it, hear it, taste it, smell it or touch it, then it doesn't exist was the lesson. This supported the "I'll believe it when I see it" mentality.

But, there are in fact many forces, elements and energies that govern our universe that are undetectable by our human senses. These unseen forces, such as gravity, magnetism, electricity, radio and TV signals, ultrasonic sound waves and ultra-violet light waves are just a few of the commonly known and acceptable invisible forces of our universe. We only sense the results of these forces. In other words, one cannot see gravity, but we feel its results. One cannot see a radio or television signal, we only see and hear the results of the signal being received.

What about our own bodies, especially our brain? A neurosurgeon can cut open a skull, probe our brain, see and feel all the physical parts of the anatomy, but a surgeon cannot see our thoughts, ideas, feelings, memories, axiological values, personality, moods, our conscious or subconscious mind, or our "soul.". They cannot see, taste, smell, hear or touch any of the elements of our being. Yet, we all have them and do not question their existence.

One of the most powerful laws of our universe is known as the Law of Attraction (LOA). The law of attraction is the power that draws similar energies together and is one of the most prolific of the universal laws. The law of attraction is the manifestation of the creative power of the Universe. It is through this law that everything is created: galaxies, planets, metals, rocks and even plants, animals and people. Even the law of gravity is part of the law of attraction. This incredible force attracts thoughts, ideas, people, situations and circumstances together that are on the same wavelength.

Our thoughts and the law of attraction are forces, manifestations of energy, that have a powerful type of attraction. It is also a principle that our human ego has struggled to accept and understand throughout time. This is mostly because it defies logic.

Whether one believes in the law of attraction or not, it is constantly present and working in all of our lives. How many times have you heard or said things like "be careful what you wish for," or "birds of a feather flock together?" I find it amusing that our ego can acknowledge the law of attraction in the negative or undesirable context, but often struggles with trusting its capabilities in a positive perspective.

The law of attraction is not just a theory. It is supported by modern science as well as every major religion in the world. It has been preached about for centuries, is well-documented in the Bible and every other religious teaching of various faiths. It is neither luck nor chance that one finds him or herself in a given situation at any given time.

It is the law of attraction that has placed us where we are in life. We do in fact co-create our reality and surroundings. If our life becomes "not to our liking", we (i.e., our egos) usually blame everyone or everything else for these undesirable results. In fact, the "blame game" mentality of our brainwashing commercial and advertising culture seems to have jumped onto the "it's not your fault" bandwagon.

There is one weight-loss TV commercial that just floors me every time I hear it:

"Are you overweight? Do you have a bulging midsection?... Excess tummy flab is not your fault!"

LOL. It's NOT YOUR FAULT? And for only $$$, their "magic little pill" will let you eat whatever you want. No need to exercise, it will simply rid you of your unsightly belly fat! Please refer back to Albert Einstein's definition of 'Insanity' in the Preface.

William Atkinson, in his book,

> *The Law of Attraction in the Thought World*, states *"A strong thought or constant thought, or dwelling on something, will make us the center of attraction for corresponding thought waves. In other words, good or bad, positive or negative, like attracts like. As the Bible puts it: 'As ye sow, so shall ye reap.'"*

Some of the most predominate and influential writings for me on LOA include the following:

William Atkinson: *The Law of Attraction in the Thought World* (1906)

Wallace Wattles: *The Science of Getting Rich* (1910)

Napoleon Hill's two best sellers: *The Law of Success* (1928) and *Think and Grow Rich* (1937) *"Whatever the mind* can conceive and believe, it can achieve."

Guy W. Ballard: *The I Am Discourses*, of Saint Germain, Volume 3 (1932-35)

Earl Nightingale: *The Strangest Secret* (1956) *"We are what we think about."*

Dr. Denis Waitley: *The Psychology of Winning:* Ten Qualities of a Total Winner (1979)

Tony Robbins: *Unlimited Power* (1987) & *Awaken the Giant within* (1991)

Esther & Jerry Hicks: *The Teachings of Abraham (1988+)*

Dr. Deepak Chopra: *The Seven Spiritual Laws of Success*: A Practical Guide to the Fulfillment of Your Dreams (1994)

Rhonda Byrne: *The Secret* (2006)

Dr. Wayne Dyer: *Wishes Fulfilled* (2012)

Biblical references to the law of attraction include:

Mathew 21:22- *(NIV)* If you believe, you will receive whatever you ask for in prayer."

Author Sen writes:

"When you ask or desire for something, and believe in your mind that you can have it, then you activate a strong current of attraction which will draw you towards its manifestation".

This is exactly what Jesus was conveying in Mathew 21:22.

The most important factor to note is the emphasis on "believe". Because when you ask for something and don't believe that you can have it. It's not possible for you to see its manifestation, because you will not be a vibrational match to your desire."

Matthew 7:7- (NIV) *"Ask, and it shall be given to you; seek, and you shall find; knock, and it shall be opened unto you."*

Mark 11:24- (NIV) "Therefore I tell you, whatever you ask for in prayer, believe that you have received it, and it will be yours."

Book after book, seminar after seminar, and verse after verse have taught us: *We are, and attract into our lives, what we think, say and believe about ourselves and our perceived reality.*

A positive mental attitude is the key to our success and happiness in life. This realization is imperative, and once truly comprehended, it is life-changing. The "steps" of this attraction are seemingly simple:

Ask, Believe and Receive.

However, the mental conditioning required to gain and maintain this positive attitude to attract, manifest and sustain a happy, abundant and prosperous life is what many consider one of life's most challenging endeavors.

I am here to tell you, my friends, that it doesn't have to be such a challenge. As previously stated, the law of attraction is a constant, and is at work in your life whether you believe in it or not.

We are, and attract into our lives, what we think, say and believe about ourselves and our perceived reality.

The process for most people, unfortunately only occurs on a subconscious level. Because they don't realize that the law of attraction is at work in their every thought, every word and every emotion, they attract many things and situations by default – some desirable but most undesirable.

This law of attraction we cannot change, but what we can change is how we use or allow it to govern our lives. Using the law of attraction in a deliberate manner is, fortunately, a conditional behavior that can be learned. However, our egos and muddled thoughts frequently create a great deal of indecision, uncertainty and disbelief. As a result, our self-imposed destructive thoughts get in our way and prevent our desires from becoming physical realities. The process is built on corresponding thought frequencies that you create and send out to the universe.

Our thoughts generate specific frequencies, or vibrations of energy, and send them into the universe. In turn, the universe returns events and experiences into our lives that support our beliefs and correspond with our emotional frequency. If you are often overwhelmed with frustrating situations causing anxiety and never-ending problems in your life, you will continue to attract these catastrophic episodes (i.e., emotional addictions) that keep provoking such feelings and circumstances.

Often when things start falling apart, it seems to spread to every aspect of our lives. It starts with one problem and then the domino effect seems to take over and the next thing we know, our whole life is in disarray!

When things start turning bad, how many times have you said something like *"Great, what else can go wrong today?"* or *"If it weren't for bad luck, I'd have no luck at all"*? And then there's the good ole Murphy's law one can always fall back on: *"Anything that can go wrong will go wrong."* This is a classic example of the law of attraction hard at work in your life, giving you exactly what you are confirming and affirming.

Fortunately, though, it works both ways. If we live and think in desirable terms, we will attract desirable results and these desirable results will cause similarly desirable outcomes in turn. The law of attraction is completely unbiased and impartial. It is nonjudgmental and does not punish or reward. It simply gives you what you ask for, even if you aren't aware of what you're asking for.

According to your thoughts, beliefs and emotional frequency, you attract and manifest whatever is in alignment with you. Therefore, when things are going great and you are experiencing desirable events and situations, you can most likely remember saying silly sayings like *"I'm on a roll now!"* or *"Watch out, the kid is hot!"* You get my drift. My point here is that when you experience pleasure in your life, you will keep attracting more blissful situations, and life is grand!

Now, I know that some of you are thinking it sounds good on paper, but it just doesn't work that way in real life. Well,

I'm here to tell you that it really does! I know and understand that we've all experienced grand events or situations in our lives only to be disappointed, let down, or discouraged by the bottom falling out from under our incredible situation. Why? Because you affirmed and attracted this undesirable result. How? By allowing fearful thoughts about losing the experience, thing or situation.

Have you ever said:

> *"I can't believe it!" "No way," "This is too good to be true," "This kind of stuff never happens to me"*?

As life goes on and we experience the gains and losses of these incredible situations, many of us adopt an automatic negative attitude when something grand and glorious finally does happen.

How many times have you said:

> *"Yeah, but just wait,"* or *"It's good now, I'm just waiting for the other shoe to drop,"* and of course there's the good ole *"Nothing this good lasts forever."*

How many times have you successfully, and usually unknowingly, attracted and manifested a great situation or experience and then turned around and attracted the loss of that same experience? Talk about the law of attraction hard at work!

For me, I have experienced this roller coaster of life more than a few times, and I finally realized that I was the cause of these so-called "failures". I say "so-called" failures because I now choose to look at every experience in my life as just that – an experience. Back then, I allowed my ego to blame everything and everyone else for all of the downs in my life. Why? Because I had worked so hard to be successful at whatever I was seeking to accomplish.

I eventually learned that when I worked that hard to be successful, once I had achieved a satisfactory level of success, I often became fearful of maintaining it and/or losing it. And it's no surprise, I lost it every time!

For those of you who know the Tony Robbins' story, mine is much the same. I have been a millionaire, I have been homeless, and then a millionaire again, and then lost it again. I have been in incredible relationships with amazing women and then lost them. I've had fantastic jobs and lost them... the list goes on. But not anymore! I finally figured out that it was me that caused these experiences. All of them. The ups and the downs. They were and are all manifested through me and my thoughts.

> *We are, and attract into our lives, what we think, say and believe about ourselves and our perceived reality.*

It is our thoughts that give our experiences meaning. I now choose not to evaluate or label a situation as good or bad. Instead, I choose to see experiences as experiences. Our reactions to our experiences are our choices. God calls it "free will." William Shakespeare puts it: "There is nothing either good or bad, but thinking makes it so." I believe all experiences are good in one way or another, and I simply refer to the outcomes as either *desirable* or *undesirable* as a result of an action.

So, how does one create and maintain a miraculous life full of happiness, abundance and prosperity? As I mentioned before, and as the law of attraction states, the answer is "easy" if you so choose.

I AM
Prepared

CHAPTER 3

I AM Prepared

Kaizen and the Miyagi coefficient

The first step to creating a desirable life of bliss, happiness and abundance is to **_believe_** you can create, or co-create, a blissful life. I say "co-create" because God is our creator and God is in all of us. Therefore, we are all a piece of God. We have also been blessed by our creator with free will and choice. Therefore, by having God dwell within us and by God giving us options, we all have the opportunity to choose and create the life we desire.

In other words, you get to choose what follows your "I AM"s and what you want to attract into your life! It really is that simple. You and your life will be as great as the thoughts and affirmations that you think and speak.

Although the concept may seem simple, what I have found through my own experiences, as well as the shared experiences of many others, is that following this "simple" philosophy can be very challenging indeed. I have also learned that these challenges are self-imposed. The good news is that in the following chapters I explain how I have learned to use the law of attraction and the influence of the divine "I AM" as I perceive it, to create a wonderful life of bliss.

My life adventures have been absolutely incredible. I learned early in life about the law of attraction and how to use it to my advantage. As a young boy, my father paid me fifty cents per week to record Earl Nightingale's five-minute radio show "Our changing world" every morning.

At this early age, I learned from my job as "Recording Engineer" that "We become what we think about," and in Sunday school, I was taught,

> "As ye sow, so shall ye reap" and *"What things so ever ye desire, when ye pray, believe that ye receive [them], and ye shall have [them]."*

Wow, what a concept! I thought, *It's like having superpowers!*

As I went through my adolescence, I would use these "secret superpowers" to get what I wanted. In those days, it was mostly material things, and it was amazing that I really could "influence" the outcome to my favor and basically get what I wanted.

As I grew older and "wiser – and I use the term "wiser" with extreme sarcasm – my secret superpowers didn't seem to work as well. Not that I couldn't manifest what I desired, but it seemed as though I couldn't hang on to what I had manifested. So I would pick myself up, dust myself off, go back to my original youthful "secret superpower" mind frame, and rebuild. Once I began to manifest my desire(s), be it material or situational, things would begin to come together again.

 Money in the bank, condo on the beach, Porsche in the garage, yadda yadda yadda, then a few years later, it suddenly falls apart leaving me broke and living in my office, again. Everything gone from what never seemed to be my own fault, my "conscious" fault that is. This cycle happened to me, or I should say I created this cycle in my life, five times!

I had many periods in between the ups and downs, frustrated, confused and soul searching, wondering "what's wrong with me?" I had become a great manifester. In fact, when things would fall apart, I would just turn up the positive self-reinforcement, tell myself "Hey, if I did it once, I can do it again!" and I did! The only thing was, there was starting to be too many "again"s. After "experience" number five, I finally realized I needed to take a more realistic look at Einstein's definition of 'insanity':

"Doing the same thing over and over again and expecting different results".

During this period of time, I learned that faith, perseverance, persistence and tenacity are what inspires one to get back up. I, like many others, have this drive. However, even though these qualities will get you back on your feet, they won't necessarily keep you from falling again.

There are countless inspiring success stories about those who have experienced the same rags-to-riches-and-back-again story that I was experiencing. Between 1832 and 1860 (that's twenty seven years), Abraham Lincoln failed at business, failed at being an attorney, has a nervous breakdown, ran for and lost the political offices of Speaker, Congress, US Senate, and Vice-President. He did have many successes in between, but talk about a long list of failures – there were twelve of them to be exact! But then in 1860, he was elected to be our 16th President of the United States, and is highly regarded as one of the most influential, history-changing Presidents ever.

Similarly, Walt Disney was fired from the newspaper he worked for and was told that "he lacked imagination and had no good ideas." Henry Ford had two failed and bankrupt automobile companies before he launched the Ford Motor Company.

There are many such stories of people who have gone through this cycle and then managed to break it and sustain the greatness they knew was within them. It was these people that inspired me to find out what they all had in common. Also, what they had adapted in their "formula" that gave them this sustaining success power.

It wasn't that the law of attraction wasn't working. It's ALWAYS working. However, once they, like myself achieved or manifested a desired goal or achievement, the fear of losing it became the dominant thought pattern. What I and these others were thinking and attracting was simply fear – the fear of failure and even sometimes the fear success.

As a youngster, my imagination and my belief that anything was possible was my true and dominant foundation. But, through my "adult wisdom", I learned about fear, lack and "losing it all" as well as allowing other "garbage" to park in my belief center.

I had learned as a young boy that "we are, and attract into our lives, what we think, say and believe about ourselves and our perceived reality."

So the cycle was to ask, believe and receive, and then once received the focus turned from abundance, gratitude and joy, to the fear of losing it. Then, as the law of attraction did its job, all would be lost. This was my cycle, and it is the case for many others. Sustaining and maintaining an abundant life is as easy or challenging as we make it.

Through these experiences, I have learned there really is no "good" or "bad", there are only experiences we have throughout our lives that we classify as such. Every event in our lives is a learning experience. We have the free will and choice to do with its outcome as we wish.

When I think back to when I was a kid with my "secret superpowers", I think of how great life was. Then, when I grew up, my superpowers got overshadowed by what I was told to believe. In a rather odd way, it reminds me of the Adam and Eve story. All was great until they ate the fruit from the tree of the knowledge of good and evil.

As I mentioned earlier, the law of attraction breaks down to ask, believe and receive. However, before you can successfully put the law of attraction to work in a positive way, you must first learn how to create a true and accepting open mind. Much like a farmer, one must first prepare the soil before planting the seeds. This includes clearing out the weeds and feeding the soil with fertilizing nutrients and water. It also includes preparing a plan of action. For the farmer, many decisions must be made before he plants the first seed, and there is a schedule he must follow throughout the cycle.

The Kaizen Coefficient

In order to effectively implement the law of attraction without being overwhelmed, I use the Kaizen system, which is the practice of continuous improvement. I use the Kaizen method on a weekly basis, so I don't overwhelm myself with too much too fast. If I wanted to start multiple new processes, exercises or behaviors such as a daily gratitude journal, meditation routine, affirmation monolog, and a list of goals, starting and maintaining all of this at once may be too much for me. However, taking one change at a time, focusing all of my energy on it and doing it for at least a week or ten days really works well for me. I do this before I add the next new behavior. One can even call this "baby steps." You can find plenty of information online about Kaizen and how to adopt a system into your routine. My main point here is that you will be making quite a few changes in your daily routine as well as within your mind, so staying organized and not getting overwhelmed will help you make these new changes in lifelong behaviors.

The Miyagi Deferential

I often think of the movie "The Karate Kid" when first teaching people the steps of successful LOA or manifestation. The reason I reference "The Karate Kid" is because you must first prepare and condition yourself before you can effectively and successfully learn and implement or manipulate the steps of the law of attraction – *ask, believe, and receive.* If you recall in the movie, before Daniel was taught any karate moves, Mr. Miyagi had him perform several unrelated tasks (with precise repetitious movements, such as painting the fence, sanding the deck, hanging up his coat, and of course the famous "wax on… wax off." The story later reveals, these movements were essential to learn first in order to effectively implement the art of karate. The same goes for learning the art of manifestation. You must first prepare your mind in order to remove the psychological blocks and negative beliefs you have created in your reality that will prevent the positive law of attraction from manifesting.

You must also learn how to effectively use your divine inner skills to co-create, grow and reap the benefits of your manifestations.

Again, I refer back to the farmer who has to clear out the weeds, prepare the soil, plant the seeds, tend to their growth and then reap the harvest. As you will soon realize, these steps are essential. Just as Daniel did not understand the "why", you must overcome any resistance that you may have about skipping over these preparatory steps.

After many years of learning and refining these steps, I am now blessed with a miraculous life of enjoyment and abundance. Each step is presented on its own, and I ask that you please take your time and work with each section faithfully, applying the principle of Kaizen, before you move on to the next.

I AM
Worthy

CHAPTER 4

I AM Worthy

Believe In Yourself

Before anything else, the next important step you must take is: You must have a rock solid, indestructible, unshakable and secure self-worth. Your own self-worth will determine whether you will succeed or fail in creating your desires in life.

As I mentioned earlier, the first step is to believe that you can create a blissful life. In order to do so, you must first feel worthy and deserving of a grand and miraculous lifestyle. Your true emotional beliefs are nestled deep within your subconscious mind and have been developed over time.

Henry Ford stated:

"Whether you think you can or think you can't, you're absolutely right."

Thinking you can't, is in my opinion, the purest and truest form of self-imposed limitations, and is caused by your lack of a sense of worth. It is the only thing that can and will hold you back. Self-imposed limitation is only caused by a lack of self-worth, self-esteem, self-image, self-confidence or however you want to label it. The bottom line is: How you feel about yourself is a choice, although it often doesn't feel that way.

The late Florence Scovel-Shinn wrote:

"The subconscious is simply power, without direction. It is like a stream of electricity, and it does what it is directed to do; it has no power of induction. Whatever man feels deeply or pictures clearly, is impressed upon the subconscious mind."

If you believe yourself to be unworthy, then somewhere in your life you were presented with the idea that you are. Eventually, this idea became a belief. Although it was a lie, perhaps you were convinced because people you trusted told you so, or perhaps circumstances confirmed it to you.

Regardless, the belief that you are unworthy was stored away in your subconscious as if it were the truth.

Now, your subconscious causes you to live in a way that confirms your lack of self-worth. The power of your subconscious mind is the reason why low self-worth can have such a destructive hold on you. It's something so ingrained in you that you unknowingly make decisions limited by the self-sabotaging deceptions of your subconscious.

You must change any and all negative thought patterns to positive thoughts and emotions about yourself and your reality. I hear people say negative things about themselves in a humorous and joking manner all the time. Things such as: "Through the lips and straight to the hips" or "Well, if it weren't for bad luck, I'd have no luck at all." Although these statements are funny, you have to realize that your subconscious mind does not know that you are just joking around. To your subconscious, this is an affirmation that it takes literally and it goes to work broadcasting the necessary thought frequencies to attract your affirmation. So, congratulations, your desires have been fulfilled... welcome that extra weight gain and bad luck! You asked for it and the universe delivered, just as you affirmed.

The change from undesirable or low-vibrational thinking to desirable, high vibrational thinking starts with you making a conscious decision to do so, and working these new positive self-beliefs deep down into your subconscious mind. You must consciously work on this until these positive emotions of self-worth are engrained as your true and honest opinions. If not, the law of attraction will stay busy at work creating your unworthy life.

For a great example of this, let's look at financial problems. Remember that your beliefs are nestled deep in your subconscious and control your beliefs about what you are worthy of and what is possible. If you believe that you can never get ahead financially or that you only deserve just enough money to barely get by, or that there's never enough, then your subconscious will emit these thought frequencies to the universe, which in turn will attract back into your life these exact situations in order to support your perceived reality.

If you are stressing about your bills, avoid the bill collectors, fighting with your spouse over money, worrying about how you're going to make your next payment, looking for solutions and feeling terrible about it, then that is the exact signal or frequency you're broadcasting to the universe. Obsessing or focusing about your financial <u>problems</u> only makes matters worse, and the more you stress over them trying to find a solution, the worse it gets because you keep attracting more negativity back into your reality.

Focus = Fuel

The more you focus on emotions such as anxiety, worry, stress, fear, hopelessness, frustration, jealousy, criticism, judgment, and doubt the more you call these negative emotions into your life, and the problem just keeps gaining momentum. It's a Catch 22, a self-fulfilling prophecy of disaster – unless you STOP this negative thought process.

Even if you are in fact sending out the exact thought frequency vibrations needed to attract something you desire, often a subconscious belief about not deserving what you are attempting to manifest will be enough to prevent the benefits from arriving. You may successfully go through the entire process of attempting to attract and create your desires, but if you don't believe in your own self-worth, consciously and especially subconsciously, then you will attract nothing but disappointment. Why? Because your deep-seeded emotional beliefs are those of unworthiness. There may be several self-inflicting negative behaviors and beliefs you have that will prevent you from achieving your desired life. So how do you change this? You have to affirm and truly believe emotionally and deeply in your subconscious mind that you are in fact worthy and deserving of a wonderful life.

The process begins with you accepting yourself for who you are, understanding your "true self", and making the most of the gifts you are blessed with. Stop being angry, resentful, jealous or feeling dejected for what you don't have.

Our modern world has brainwashed us so intensely through marketing that we've been brought up being told and believing we are NOT good enough until we have "X" product, whatever that may be at the moment. This is your ego façade busy at work for you. It could be a brand of clothing, shoes, handbags, watches, cars, a hairstyle, makeup or even a cell phone. We're also told that we're going to get sick and stay unhealthy unless we take "X", or if we have "these" symptoms we need to talk to our doctor about "X" disease for a prescription to control it. And don't forget, "you're going to be too tired to make it through the day unless you drink "X" super energizer drink!"

The truth is, none of these things matter, and they have absolutely no relation to your actual value and your sense self-worth. So STOP believing these brainwashing lies that are nothing but marketing tactics, which tell you (i.e., your ego) what you should look, act and sound like in order to be acceptable. They simply are not true.

The truth is, your entire existence is one of worthiness. You are a perfect child of God and are deserving of a beautiful life, simply because you're a human being who has the ability to do good in the world. Be happy, thankful and proud of who you are, your "true self", and what you actually do have.

We've all had our struggles in life, and it doesn't matter what has happened in your past. That is behind you. It is your choice to move forward and reprogram your subconscious to rid yourself of these thoughts and behaviors of low self-worth. Florence Scovel-Shinn, in her book *The Game of Life and How to Play it*, suggests going to the root of where this negative belief began.

Perhaps it was during your childhood, your marriage, first job, or a party in college. Visualize that moment in your mind. Then confront it. Be bold, speak out loud,

"Although this moment happened to me, the belief I made about myself is not true. It is a lie.

The truth is (*fill in an awesome comment about yourself here*)."

Think it. Speak it. Shout it. Every day. It takes time, frequent correction and consistency.

I suggest you write down and then affirm out loud:

"I am _____.

Anything conflicting with this statement is a lie."

The following are suggested adjectives to fill in the blank

> **Worthy, Deserving, Confident, Valuable, Loving, Lovable, Smart, Beautiful, Funny, Honest, Strong, Secure, Courageous, Successful, A Winner, The Best, Interesting, Respected, Friendly, Kind, Compassionate, Forgiving, A Wonderful Person, Always Positive, and Secure in Who I AM.**

Remember, good or bad:

We are, and attract into our lives, what we think, say and believe about ourselves and our perceived reality.

Make a list of at least 10 of these affirmations and repeat them over and over, especially in the morning and most importantly, just as you go to sleep.

Your subconscious is simply doing its job of storing information and guiding you based upon images, experiences, information and beliefs. You are in control of the information it receives.

Your life is too valuable to waste on lies, and no one can convince you of your worthiness other than you. It is entirely your choice. You are a child of God, a unique and priceless human being. This marvel in and of itself makes you worthy of every opportunity to experience a life filled with the abundance of anything you desire. All you have to do is decide to believe it and then live it.

As I mentioned at the start of this chapter, a strong, unshakable and an indestructible sense of high self-worth is the foundation of creating your desired life and manifesting anything you want. As with anything that is built, it must have a very strong and sturdy foundation that is both deep and wide. It is your life and your choice. You now have the necessary tools, so start building your foundation of worthiness.

I AM
Happy

CHAPTER 5

I AM Happy

Sustain True Happiness

"Happiness doesn't depend on any external conditions; it is governed by our mental attitude."
Dale Carnegie

"Now and then it's good to pause in our pursuit of happiness and just be happy."
Guillaume Apollinaire

What is happiness? Please take a moment after reading this paragraph to stop reading and answer the question. I encourage you to write it down, or at least verbally state your definition out loud. There is no right or wrong answer. Your personal definition of happiness, which is embedded in your subconscious, actually plays a key role in your life and your approach, or attitude toward how you live. Now, when I say "answer", I don't mean a textbook answer. I mean a heartfelt answer of what happiness truly means to you, from your "true" self. The honest "you." The "you" that doesn't need a title, or a reputation, or 'enhanced" hair, boobs, lips, nose or whatever. Not the "you" that can only be seen in the latest designer clothes, shoes, or jewelry. The real you, that doesn't need a fancy car. The real "you", who is just..."you". I ask you to do this in order to open your mind and start learning to think from your "true self", and to help clarify what happiness means to you.

Please stop reading right now, ponder and write down your answer to:

"What is happiness?"

It is well documented that, when asked "What do you want?" most people worldwide answer "happiness." This is also the most popular answer when parents are asked what they want most for their children. It is widely accepted and understood that happiness is the driving force behind many of our life goals, such as success, prosperity, wellness and loving relationships.

What I find most amazing is that when you ask someone to define happiness, many people are at a loss for an answer. They either answer with the textbook or dictionary definition or their ego answers the question for them. Your ego is not your true self and many people have found that their ego will actually keep them from the very thing(s) they desire. Your ego is a psychological façade and is constantly trying to convince you that it knows best in order to keep you from psychological harm. The ego has no trust or faith, and lives mainly in the past, and although it thinks it is helping you, it is really just trying to survive.

Happiness is actually our natural state of being and is something that we already are and always will be; yet, many people spend much of their lives seeking happiness. Does this sound familiar?

"I will be happy when _____."

Happiness is not an external "thing" that you can get, buy, earn, or find. It is not a byproduct of achievement.

Happiness is what I define as an essence of being. I have learned that happiness truly is something that we already "are." Think of "happiness" as the sun. On a cloudy day, we commonly, yet erroneously say "the sun is not shining today." But the sun is, in fact, shining. The sun is always shining; we just don't see it from where we are because a cloud blocks its rays. When we choose to move out from under the cloud, we are once again in the sunshine. If you are not living in happiness, you have the option to stay where you are, or move out from under the cloud, so to speak, and into happiness.

Happiness is often defined and classified into groups of threes, such as *Pleasant, Engaged* and *Meaningful,* or *Pleasant, Circumstantial* and *Joyful,* and even *Tamasic, Rajasic* and *Sattvic.*

1. *Pleasure.* Defined as sensory happiness, pleasure is a neurochemical endorphin response to stimuli of one of our physical senses. Sensory happiness is wonderful in that we have the ability to experience incredible pleasures through sight, sound, taste, touch and smell. Unfortunately, sensory pleasure has its dark side, where good can often turn bad. Sensory pleasure is temporary and needs a stimulus, which often leads to addiction. But, if enjoyed responsibly, we can truly relish the pleasure we receive from this type of happiness.

2. *Circumstantial Happiness:* This type of happiness is achieved through the satisfaction of getting what we want, or being happy because of various circumstances, past and present, that occur in our life. Happiness, fulfillment, and contentment are derived from circumstances such as career satisfaction, relationship satisfaction, and life satisfaction.

Circumstantial happiness is usually expressed by saying such things as:

"I am happy because _____."

This type of happiness is very uplifting, but, like its cousin Pleasure, circumstantial happiness needs a stimulus, in the form of an achievement or milestone. It can be a great motivation tool, though, as circumstantial happiness is often very short-lived.

For example, the celebration of an achievement, such as a job promotion, soon dies out as our focus quickly turns toward the next level of advancement. Throughout life we enjoy our accomplishments and achievements but never seem to be satisfied with them. Remember your first job, your first car, your first house, your first computer, your first… anything? They were all good, but soon, they were no longer enough. I suggest you relish and celebrate your accomplishments. Enjoy the moment – you deserve it!

3. *True Happiness:* The seemingly elusive beast. The lifelong dream of dreams. True bliss. The state of being happy for no reason other than to be happy. The concept first seems very difficult to grasp as we have been conditioned, mainly through marketing and advertising, to feel that we need a reason to be happy, and that X product will be what brings us happiness.

True happiness is already a part of you and always will be. It is your choice to live your life being happy all the time, or succumb to the conditional elements of "marketed" happiness.

Through my own experiences, I have found this state of happiness, and it feels fantastic! I AM happy, just because! Because I am a child of God! Because I am me! Because I am that I am. Because I CHOOSE to be happy, all the time!

Remember, like attracts like, and we (our lives) are that which we think about most. You must train yourself to constantly be and stay happy all the time in order to emulate and receive this higher level of beingness or energy. And just when you're at the peak of happiness, try to learn how to be even happier.

There are countless books written on the subject of happiness and I have found that they can all be summarized with:
Happiness is a choice, and to be happy, one must simply choose to be happy.

That conclusion, in and of itself, I agree wholeheartedly with, but again, I must say it is easier said than done.

So let's take a closer look at how we can train ourselves to be and stay happy. On a scientific level, the physical and emotional act of being happy releases serotonin, endorphins, dopamine and other feel-good indicators throughout our body. In fact, just the simple act of smiling releases endorphins! Yes, that's right!

When your mouth and face muscles create a smile, your brain reacts to the smile by saying "Yippee, we are happy about something, let's party!" The happy juices begin to flow, your thought vibrations increase, and you are now attracting on this higher plane. So starting right now, I want you to smile, and keep smiling! Start a "smile routine" where every hour you remind yourself to smile for at least one minute. As a great training aid, get a #2 yellow pencil, open your mouth as wide as you can, place the pencil horizontally in your mouth touching the corners of your mouth and then lightly bite down on it holding it in place with your teeth. This will physically stimulate the same muscle sequence known as smiling, which will send the "party time" happy signal to your brain and voila, now you're feeling the neurochemical reaction! This part of your brain has no perceptive thought process only a neuro-biochemical reaction response to the muscular stimulation.

Remember, according to the law of attraction, like attracts like. Being happy will attract more happiness to your life. It is a choice that you and only you can make. When undesirable events happen in our life, we are often required to make decisions in order to adjust, rectify or essentially "handle" the situation. All too often, it is the wrong time to try to make any critical decisions. Why? Because at this time we are in a very low state of vibrational energy due to our emotional response to the situation. This is probably the worst time to try to evaluate and assess.

The best thing you can do for yourself and all others involved is to first physically remove yourself from the situation if possible and then do something that will increase your vibrational (positive) energy. In other words, go to your proverbial "happy place." In order to think rationally and make critical decisions, you have to be in a higher state of being, and this will help you get there. Remember that like attracts like. We attract into our lives, what we think about most.

Think for a moment on a larger scale – think of our world leaders who have to deal with incredibly tragic and often devastating situations all the time. Now ask yourself – when these types of undesirable situation happen, where do we find our leaders? Usually they're anywhere but at ground zero. Why? Because they know and understand that attempting to make decisions concerning a crisis while in the middle of the crisis is a bad idea. Like attracts like, and being emotionally overwhelmed in a tragic situation only attracts more emotional and mental or psychological turmoil.

It is for this reason that leaders are often found on a retreat while the rest of the world is fed a steady stream of minute-by-minute devastation and tragedy on TV, radio and the Internet. As a whole, we often get sucked into the human emotion of a situation. Whether it's happening around the corner, several miles away or on the other side of the world, our media is so incredibly good at making us feel like we're right there. So, in your mind, it's like you are there and it's happening directly to you.

Congratulations, drama kings and queens, you are now personally in the middle of the crisis. Your emotions are off the chart with dismay, shock, alarm, anger, depression and hopelessness. You think "everyone else in the world surely MUST feel this same way, and anyone who doesn't is a sick, disgusting, and heartless beast." Then, to make matters even worse, the media outrages you by flaunting the fact that during all of this devastation, your "leaders" are on vacation. On vacation in the middle of a tragedy? And of course the media has a field day and targets your emotions once again. "Ah, the audacity" you think or say. "How dare they go on vacation and hide from the situation when my world is in a crisis?"

I understand that this is a very challenging pill to swallow, and as sordid as it may seem, I fully understand why. One can be far more focused and rational when solving a problem or dealing with a crisis from a distance, both physically and emotionally. This is also the same reason why physicians are told not to treat their family members.

Your life goal should be:

Be happy no matter what the outside stimulus.

It is often stated that life is full of ups and downs, good times and bad times, easy times and hard times. I don't fully agree with those statements – I firmly believe that all times are "good" times because there is always something good that comes out of every situation. I call them "desirable" and "undesirable" outcomes. Being broke and happy is much better than being broke and miserable. Face it, at that moment, being happy or miserable is your choice. When you're broke and happy, you have a much better chance of attracting prosperity than if you're angry, depressed and feeling like a victim.

Many people have already decided how happy they will allow their lives to be on a daily, weekly, yearly or even a lifetime basis. This happiness allowance can be changed at any time, but it can only be changed by you, and the change can only come from within. This transformation only happens when one stops searching for happiness and chooses to enjoy the feeling of joy within themselves.

Robert Holden states:
"There is a world of difference between searching for happiness and following your joy. Following your joy is about listening to your heart's desires, noticing what truly inspires you and recognizing your soul's purpose.

A good starting point is to reflect on the question 'When am I at my happiest?' People who follow their joy discover a depth of talent and creativity that inspires all of us."

Choose to be happy no matter what. Even if you are faced with an undesirable situation, choose to be and stay happy. It will get you through the situation much better and faster. *Like attracts like. We are, and attract into our lives, what we think, say and believe about ourselves and our perceived reality.*

Earlier in the chapter, I suggested that you "go to your happy place." This is a state of mind that can bring you back into your full shining happiness. Going to your happy place is a very effective way to cope with undesirable situations; it will help keep your vibrational energy at a higher level. To be honest, I have learned that you really need to create not just one, but several happy places to really make this option effective. I personally have eight of them – all fantastic. Your happy place does not have to be the Hollywood-style dream of some fantasy land that is entirely made-up in your mind. It can and, in my opinion, should be something or someone that is, has been, or will be experienced in your reality.

To begin creating your happy place, you need to get out your notebook/journal and start writing down things that make you happy. Start with past events from as far back as you can remember. Think of the great experiences you had growing up, like going to Disneyland, camping, or going to the beach on vacation. How about the carnival or the circus? Maybe your favorite birthday party or favorite Christmas or holiday season. How about your favorite TV show, movie or game you used to play for hours on end? Write all of these down as you think of them, and we'll sort through them later. Who were your favorite friends when you were young, and what did you guys do for fun? Did you have any pets? Think of the fun times you had with your dog or cat, hamster, guinea pig, or bird. Did you ever visit a farm or ranch? Who were some of your favorite relatives? Think of specific events and situations that really ignited all of your senses.

For example, my grandfather was a tile mason and when he was pulling into their long driveway he would always honk the horn. I would run out to his work truck, jump into his lap and he would let me drive (i.e., hold on to the steering wheel) from the end of the driveway to the back of their property where his workshop was located. He always made me feel so important and would seemingly hang on every word I said as I told him about my day's adventure. He would then greet my grandmother and retire to his recliner. Grandma would bring him a glass of beer, which he would enjoy while puffing on his pipe. Still to this day, I can vividly see him, hear him, smell his beer and his pipe, which he lit with a wooden match. I can also feel the heartfelt love I received from him – such a wonderful man.

I have countless memories of him that can instantly put a smile in my heart, but sitting on his lap and "driving" the truck is by far the most memorable.

Take my suggestion about your childhood memories and do the same with your teen years, and then your adulthood (past and present) adding as many happy events, situations and people as you can. Next, you may also create fictional futuristic happy events, situations and people as well. We will discuss this option in further detail later in the book when we further discuss the imagination and visualization, but if you are able to create these imaginative happy places at this time, by all means go for it!

Once you have completed this step, you can then begin to pare it down to your top six, or your top ten or twelve "Go-to Happy Places". Once you have them chosen, start filling in as many details as possible using all of your senses. Write them down in detail in your journal. And don't forget to do the pencil smile as well. You may also use props, mementos and photographs to help remind you of your happy places, such as a sea shell for a beach experience, or a piece of tree bark for a camping trip.

Congratulations, you now officially have your happy places. Remember, keeping a half-dozen or so of them on hand is very effective because if one doesn't seem to work, just go to the next one on the list. Keep thinking of new ones, keep building your list and think of them often, not just when you're in an undesirable situation. These are your private inner spaces and places to go where you can enjoy your true shining, smiling, and happy self. A place you should be all the time!

You may also make a list of enjoyable activities that can bring you joy and even laughter. Your list should include your favorite movies, TV shows, and books. You may also include fun activities that you enjoy like cooking, gardening, arts & crafts, sewing, needlepoint, woodworking, dancing and singing. The list is endless. Write these down and gather the items needed to enjoy these mood shakers. I absolutely love listening to a stand-up comedian named Brian Regan. This man makes me laugh like no one else! I have all of his routines recorded into my iPod, and I am armed to start laughing at a moment's notice. I also enjoy playing guitar and always have one close at hand to start playing whenever I need to give my mind a break. In fact, while writing this book, I have spent a lot of time strumming the ole six-string, plus I have written three new songs. My point here is, you sometimes need to have a collection of "go-to activities" to help you reach your happy places. Your number-one goal is to be and stay happy all the time! Smile, smile, smile and stay in a happy frame of mind all the time. Soon you will notice the proverbial cloud of doom and gloom disappear, and your true self will spread happiness throughout your heart and the hearts of those around you. Remember, everyone brightens up a room – some do it when they walk in, and others when they walk out. Which one do you want to be?

I AM
Grateful

CHAPTER 6

I AM Grateful

Living every moment with the powerful

Attitude of Gratitude

"Acknowledging the good that you already have in your life is the foundation for all abundance."

— Eckhart Tolle

"Some people grumble that roses have thorns; I am grateful that thorns have roses."

— Alphonse Karr

"When you are grateful, fear disappears and abundance appears."

— Anthony Robbins

"Whatever you appreciate and give thanks for will increase in your life."

— Sanaya Roman

"The only people with whom you should try to get even are those who have helped you."

— John E. Southard

I just had to begin this section with some of my favorite quotes on gratitude. Why? To show my gratitude to these great people and the wisdom they share. I have burned these quotes into my brain and have repeated them countless times over the years. I live my life by these quotes, and I am very grateful for the way they have shown and the hope they have given me to choose to alter my way of living.

I've heard it, read it and one hundred percent believe that gratitude is the shortest path to happiness. The more grateful you are, the happier you will feel, and sincere gratitude also opens the door to abundance! Yes, you read it correctly! If you want to attract incredibly desirable things into your life, start by showing your gratitude, love and appreciation to all the people and things you already have around you. I don't mean a one-time "thanks", or a weekly, monthly or annual "Thanksgiving" appreciation speech or acknowledgement list.

It is a daily, hourly, minutely – okay, that's not a real word, but you get my point – thing. Your display of gratitude is an ongoing way of life. Remember, like attracts like and the more you show your gratitude and appreciation, the more you will be appreciated.

Gratitude is becoming a very hot topic these days as its power is becoming increasingly evident. Religions and philosophers have always taught about the power of gratitude, but the scientific world is now catching up. Dr. Robert Emmons from UC Davis is on the cutting edge of scientific research on gratitude. He states that gratitude is the "forgotten factor" in happiness research. Dr. Emmons and his research partner Michael McCullough, at the University of Miami, have achieved several important findings about gratitude. They've discovered scientific proof that when people regularly cultivate gratitude, they experience a variety of measurable benefits: psychological, physical, and social. In some cases, people have even reported that gratitude led to transformative life changes.

More importantly, the family, friends, partners, and others who surround them consistently report that people who practice gratitude seem significantly happier and are more pleasant to be around. Doctor's Emmons and McCollough concluded that gratitude is one of the few attitudes that can measurably change peoples' lives. Grateful people experience fewer physical ailments, such as headaches, stomachaches, nausea, and even acne. They report being less lonely, stressed, anxious and depressed.

There is nothing that amplifies your vibration and lifts your spirits faster than gratitude.

Health and Wellness Coach Ellen G. Goldman states:

> "Although we may acknowledge gratitude's benefits, it can still feel difficult to feel grateful when we are going through a difficult time. That's why it makes so much sense to *practice* gratitude, in good times and bad. It may be human nature to notice all that is wrong or that we lack, but if we give ourselves the chance on a regular basis to notice all of life's gifts and blessings, we can increase our sense of well-being, and create hope and optimism for the future—no matter what is going on."

Here are some ways to start practicing gratitude to improve your well-being. See the Gratitude Section in the I AM Journal.

1. **Keep a gratitude journal.** At the beginning and end of each day, write down 3-5 things from the day you feel grateful for. Simplicity is key. Your baby's smile, a perfect sunset, the train arriving on time, or your best friend's laughter. Relish the feeling you get when remembering and write it down.
2. **Express your gratitude.** Take the time to share your feelings. Not the simple, polite "thank you" but the

heartfelt emotions. Tell your friend how her support and sense of humor helps you get through tough times, and how much it means to you. Don't take your loved ones for granted. Let them know how much you love them and why.

3. **Look for what is right about a situation, not what's wrong.** Sure, you're frustrated that the bus arrived late, but thankfully your boss in very understanding. Sure, the service at the restaurant is poor, but you are lucky to afford an evening out surrounded by good friends.

4. **Practice gratitude with your family and friends.** Although you may not say grace before a meal, encourage each family member to report one thing that happened that day that they feel grateful for. When you hear a friend moaning and complaining, challenge him or her to find the hidden opportunity or silver lining to the situation.

So even on your most challenging days, you need to show gratitude for the pleasant things around you. When challenged, go back to the most basic or generalized statements, such as "I am grateful to breathe without having to think about it," or something along those lines.

Once you get into the routine of finding and showing gratitude for everything, it really does become a "life-changing" outlook. Start your gratitude journal today and keep it going no matter what. Find a way to remind yourself in the morning, maybe by putting a yellow sticky note next to your coffee pot and one on the bathroom mirror. You can even keep your journal next to your bed and put a yellow sticky note on your alarm clock. This way, it will be the first and last thing you do every day. It really, really works!

I AM
Thought
Energy

CHAPTER 7

I AM Thought Energy

Your vibrational energy

Everything is energy and that's all there is to it. Match the frequency of the reality you want and you cannot help but get that reality. It can be no other way. This is not philosophy. This is physics.

- Unknown

It followed from the special theory of relativity that mass and energy are both but different manifestations of the same thing.

- Albert Einstein

Now for your lesson in quantum physics! Okay, maybe not a full lesson, but let's take a moment to consider what is called "thought energy" or "thought vibrations." All physical reality is made up of vibrational energy. But, surprising to many, our thoughts have vibrational energy as well. Simply put, our brain is both a transmitter and a receiver of thought energy, or thought vibrations.

Again, we go back to the ole five-senses rule that we were taught to use as our BS meter, but please remember there are several vibrational energies that are transmitted outside of your human sensory receptors. Much like ultrasonic frequencies, infrared light, and magnetic force fields, thought vibrations are, and have been scientifically proven to be, an amazing phenomena that functions outside of our sensory spectrum.

EVERYTHING in its purest and most basic form is comprised of energy that constantly emits a frequency. We all transmit, and receive, with our thoughts. Harnessing and using this energy to our favor is the task at hand. You don't have to know or even understand the "how" of thought vibrations, you simply need to understand that this energy is yours to use in a controlled way.

Think of electricity. Most of us have no idea "how" it really works, we just plug something in, flip a switch, and it works! What about a radio, television, the Internet or your cell phone? We just use them and don't think of "how" they function. Knowing, believing and controlling thought vibrations is, in my opinion, the most critical element of the law of attraction.

Your thought energy determines what you attract and experience in every facet of your life. Whether it happens consciously or not, like attracts like. By broadcasting (and receiving) specific thought frequencies, you broadcast into the universe and then attract the necessary people, places, situations, opportunities, circumstances and things into your reality in order to physically manifest your desired result.

Remember, like attracts like and the more emotion and feelings you put into your thought, the stronger these vibrations will be and the quicker they will translate into the physical realm.

Thought vibrations are typically measured on a high-to-low scale. This can also be presented on a positive–negative scale as well. I use Dr. David Hawkins' levels of consciousness scale as my thought vibration scale:

- 700-1000: Enlightenment
- 600: Peace
- 540: Joy
- 500: Love
- 400: Reason
- 350: Acceptance
- 310: Willingness
- 250: Neutrality
- 200: Courage
- 175: Pride
- 150: Anger
- 125: Desire
- 100: Fear
- 75: Grief
- 50: Apathy
- 30: Guilt
- 20: Shame

I believe that one must always stay above 350 at all times, and I do mean all times. It must become a way of life! I am constantly aware of the level of my thought vibrations, and my personal goal is to stay above 500. When and if I ever begin an undesirable thought, either verbally or mentally, I catch myself, stop, and DO NOT finish the thought. I immediately turn it around and create a desirable thought.

I feel that when you're functioning at your higher level of thought energy, you're thinking is vibrant, optimistic and intense. Your entire being feels great! You're on top of the world!

When you function on your high vibrational level, you notice that most people, and even animals, respond well to you. You're not inclined to encounter many issues or problems, and you may even stumble upon a bit of good luck that you wouldn't normally expect. When operating from a higher level of thought vibration, people may subconsciously pick up on the fact that you are giving out that which the Beach Boys sang about:

"Good Vibrations!"

Equally, when you function at a lower frequency of thought, you're giving out bad vibes. You feel sorry for yourself, go over things that have already happened, you feel miserable and depressed, and emotions like anger, fear and discontent are the norm. People will subconsciously avoid you, or will be drawn into conflict with you. This is not a nice way to live, yet many people do live this way for the majority of their existence.

Stay very conscious of your thoughts and check yourself regularly, as in every hour. I used to set an alarm on my watch. Okay, nowadays you would do this on your cell phone. Anyway, set an alarm reminder to stop what you are doing and see where your day is going and find out what your thought vibrations are. This is very effective. The key is to train your thinking to stay at a high vibrational frequency. Like attracts like, and the world is yours to manifest whatever it is that you desire. "For as he thinketh in his heart, so is he." (Proverbs 23:7).

I AM
Perceptually Programmed

CHAPTER 8

I AM Perceptually Programmed

Using the powerful forces of your conscious and subconscious mind.

The more intensely we feel about an idea or a goal, the more assuredly the idea, buried deep in our subconscious, will direct us along the path to its fulfillment.

- Earl Nightingale

Your mind, or the function thereof, works on two levels – your conscious and subconscious mind… that's a no-brainer… (pun intended). These two levels of consciousness work in conjunction with one another to perform tasks throughout our lives. These are not two separate minds as some people teach, but two extremes of the same mind, your mind. Your conscious mind is like the control panel, with all the senses needed to gauge, test, evaluate, ponder, negotiate, and make decisions as to what is and will be the foundation of your thoughts, beliefs, lifestyle and overall persona. Your conscious thought process is ever-changing as you go through life and encounter new experiences.

Your subconscious mind, on the other hand, is the raw power that carries out the task. Once it is given an order from your conscious mind, it goes to work. It gathers, manipulates manifests and uses whatever resources it needs in order to complete the task. I have heard many different analogies over the years, but for me the simplest parallel is that of an electrical appliance. Take a microwave oven, for example – the desired task is to heat something.

First, you punch in information using the control panel regarding your desired outcome, such as cooking time, or item and weight, and then you hit start. The information is transferred to the power source and it unbiasedly follows the directions, creating the amount of energy it was told to create and sustaining it for the mandated amount of time. After the task is completed, the result may or may not be what you desired.

On a mechanical level, the microwave oven was objectively programmed and it subjectively followed through with the task it was told to accomplish. Of course, a microwave oven is incapable of logic; it simply carries out the orders and completes the tasks it is given. Your mind(s) operates on the same principle. The conscious mind is just like the microwave's control panel, providing optional input and programming information; your subconscious mind works like the power supply, carrying out the orders it receives from your conscious mind.

Remember your subconscious mind doesn't know when you're joking, it simply follows orders. Once your conscious mind believes and accepts something as a true desire, the information is transferred to your subconscious mind and will now be saved and used as a set of directions that are printed into your operating manual.

So if you say, "Every winter, I get the flu." Your subconscious creates and manifests the flu for you. If you say, "Every time I eat onion rings, I get heartburn." Then your subconscious will inform your body to create heartburn whenever you eat onion rings. It's like the conscious mind is the boss and the subconscious mind is the employee that's being told,

"Hey, the boss says it's time to get heartburn."

The subconscious mind is a follower, not a leader and a very good one at that!

Now, the cool thing about this whole conscious/subconscious thing is that it is totally controlled by you! You decide what to believe, what to desire, what orders to program your subconscious mind with, and you are the one who decides what, how and when to edit or re-program information that is already stored in your subconscious mind. In other words, you can update the operating manual and add new features whenever you desire. This is done by programming and re-programming old beliefs. This may be a challenge for some to do, but this is where your "I am" affirmations are very effective.

I AM
Imaginative

CHAPTER 9

I AM Imaginative

Gods most precious gift to man

"Whatever the mind of man can conceive and bring itself to believe, it can achieve."

- Napoleon Hill

"Here's the key to success and the key to failure: We become what we think about."
- Earl Nightingale

"Imagination is more important than knowledge. Knowledge is limited. Imagination encircles the world."

- Albert Einstein

Now for the most important tool of mankind! Everything ever created, invented, produced, formed, made, developed, refined, perfected, or designed originated from one thing – the human imagination. Anything and everything one can ever possibly want, need or desire in life must first be manifested in our imagination. Your imagination is your very own world where anything and everything is not only possible, but also a true reality that you create, develop and control. It is your kingdom to rule and nobody can stop you or tell you what you should or should not imagine. You and you alone choose how to implement your imagination and where the boundaries, if any, lay. As with the physical universe, your imagination goes to infinity and beyond! Sorry, I just had to write that.

The research and development department, commonly known as 'R&D', is where every company or business idea begins. It is the "think tank" where new ideas and thoughts are discussed, imagined and decided upon. Your imagination is your very own R&D department! As Neapolitan Hill so famously stated "Whatever the mind can conceive and believe, it can achieve."

To get started on your imagination, integration program, there are a few things you can do to waken this underutilized gift. One of the first things you can do for yourself is to remember. Remember back to when you were a young child. Remember how fun it was to use your imagination. Your current age makes no difference. Think back to when you used your imagination to create adventures like making a pillow and blanket fort or castle, or turning an ordinary box into a spaceship. Remember when you pretended you were a king or a queen, a famous movie star or famous singer! Remember how fun it was to imagine! You would imagine all kinds of incredible things to be and do. Take your journal out now and spend a few minutes remembering and writing down some of the things you imagined back in those days.

Another fun thing to do to really spark your imagination is to go outside, sit or lay down and stare at the clouds. Soon you'll start seeing all sorts of things, and the longer you stare, the funnier it gets. The more you use your imagination at this elementary level, the easier it is to start using it to uncover hidden desires.

When I was young I wanted to be a rock star. Santa brought me my first guitar when I was in fourth grade and it was the best Christmas EVER! Even though I didn't know how to play, I would set up a makeshift microphone in front of the full length mirror, put on a Beatles or Beach Boys album, grab my ax guitar, run onto the stage (in front of the mirror) and for the next hour, I was a rock star! I remember I would talk to the other band members before the show about the set list and about how many girls were out there screaming for us. Then after the show, we would have to run off the stage because the crowd would go crazy and the girls would all start chasing us. It was fun and exciting, and in my imagination, it was real!

Well, after spending countless hours, days, weeks, months, and even years playing records over and over to learn the guitar parts, I was fortunate enough to play in various garage bands throughout my high school years, bar bands in my young adulthood and finally even play professionally! I even played in a rock band on TV for a while! And to bring the Law of Attraction into full recognition here, I even got to work with some of the actual Beach Boys!
We are, and attract into our lives, what we think, say and believe about ourselves and our perceived reality.

Still to this day, I set aside some "fun time" to use my imagination. I'm still very active with music, and I still have my home "rock concerts" just as I did as a young boy in from of the mirror. The only difference from those days is that I now really do play the guitar, and I'm usually kicked back in my recliner while I'm actually playing, but in my imagination, I'm still up on that stage rocking out in front of thousands of screaming fans!

I AM
The Life I Desire

CHAPTER 10

I AM The Life I Desire

Defining your true desires

"Whatever the mind can conceive and believe, it can achieve."

— Napoleon Hill

"Whatever we plant in our subconscious mind and nourish with repetition and emotion will one day become a reality."

- Earl Nightingale

Your desire is square one, the cornerstone, the foundation, the very beginning of the journey toward all of your achievements, accomplishments and attainments. An old Chinese proverb states: "A journey of a thousand miles begins with a single step." Before you can take that very first step, you have to decide where you'd like to go. The toughest question in the world for many people is "What are your life's desires?" Not wishes or hopes, but the true desires and passions that exceed everything else in your life.

At this point in the process, in many workshops and LOA courses, you are asked to take out a sheet of paper and start writing down everything your heart desires. Some go as far as telling you to think as if you're ordering from a catalog or as if you have your own personal magic genie. Although I understand the concept, I also feel that this approach is only the first part of finding your true desires.

During this process of discovering one's true desires, it is, metaphorically speaking, very common to jump right up onto Santa's lap and start reading off your list all the neat things you want that will make your life the best ever! Don't worry, we all do that. It's how our society taught us to respond, and there is absolutely nothing undesirable about that at all.

So, I ask you now to go ahead and write down all the things you desire in your life, and yes please jump up on Santa's lap and go crazy! Have some fun and get those creative juices flowing. Your list can and should include anything and everything you desire, from material possessions to events, adventures, and situations. The only thing I ask is that you leave a few lines of blank space between each desire.

Stop reading here and write your list.

WRITE YOUR LIST IN OUR JOURNAL OR NOTEBOOK

Great, now that you have your list completed, it's time to answer the next question. If you thought the first question was a doozy, here's the next question. Why? Yes, the question is simply: why? Use the space you left between each desire to write down why this is one of your life's desires.

Stop reading again and write your answers.

In my experience, there are two types of answers – a truly heartfelt reason why, and a reason that seems more acquisitive or egocentric. If you can't feel it in your heart and soul, then it may be an ego-driven desire. Now you can use this information to learn a little more about yourself, what motivates you, and, of course, why.

I don't want to give the ending away, but through my experiences and those of countless others whom I have studied and observed, once you strip away all the ego-driven, superficial and/or society-induced brainwashing and programmed reasons, you will find that the core reason for your true desires is to be happy and to spread and share that joy with others.

Now, this is where it really starts to get exciting! You've learned that happiness is the ultimate quest in life and the key reason that motivates us to do just about everything we do. So, asking "What are your life's desires" is really the same as asking: "What influences your happiness?"

Pay close attention to this part. As we have already learned, we already are happy. It is already a part of our being. As you have read in the previous chapter, happiness is always with you, it just gets clouded over from time to time, like how we say on a cloudy day, "the sun is not shining." The sun is always shining, just as your happiness is. So if you are already happy, why do you desire the things on your list? To me, this is the key, the secret ingredient! And the answer is: "You don't need them to make you happy!" When you "need" something, you are informing and convincing your inner self, or subconscious, as well as the universe and your higher power that you are choosing to feel or "be" incomplete or in a state of lacking something.

When we feel this way, we broadcast and therefore receive on a low vibrational plane; we will continue to feel the sense of lack and our present reality follows suit to keep us in that state of lack. Why? Because this is where our mindset is and where we are transmitting our energy. But when we realize that we don't "NEED" this or that to make us happy, we can freely enjoy life with or without said desire in the physical realm, and still be happy.

Now, as confusing as this may sound, it really does eventually make sense. As you learn more and more about the strength of your influence on the law of attraction, the more you realize how vitally important it is to keep your thoughts and actions on a high vibrational plane.

The second key to this theory is to stay on your high vibrational plane. There are many names or labels for this "state of being-ness." Some call it "the zone," others call it the "vortex," and I often hear it referred to as "divine synchronicity." Call it what you will, it all boils down to the same meaning and the same state of mind; it is a level of consciousness you should learn to live in all the time. In challenging situations, perception often collapses or gets confusing, and it's tempting at those times to lose sight and revert back to a low-vibrational thought process. As tempting as this may be, choose instead to stay strong on a high vibrational plane. You are free to change your thinking anytime you desire! It's just a matter of how you choose to live your reality and when you choose to shift your thought process to a higher plane.

I believe Tony Robbins once said that to make a choice and take action on that choice only takes a millisecond, it's getting to the decision to make that change that people often drag out.

As stated many times over throughout historic teachings, everything in our physical world is first manifested in an imaginary or a vibrational plane or world. From there, things manifest in the physical plane. Therefore, once we learn to enjoy our life in the visionary plane, we really don't "need" it to manifest into the physical in order to enjoy it. By doing so, we only project high vibrational emotions toward the desire and don't transmit any feelings of lack.

We are blessed with a physical world and the power to manifest our desires into the physical realm in order to enhance and share our pleasures and happiness. Once this concept is realized, you can flourish in your high vibrational or visionary reality within your imagination and truly feel the joy and happiness that the desire stimulates. Once you learn to maintain this high vibrational level of being, you will be presented with opportunities to take action that will manifest your desires in your physical reality.

I AM Now Asking

Chapter 11

I AM Now Asking

Ask and It Shall Be Given

Ask, and you will receive. Search, and you will find. Knock, and the door will be opened for you.

- Matthew 7:7

The fine art of asking is definitely a learned process that gets developed and refined over the course of our lives. When it comes to the law of attraction and universal, higher or divine powers, the art of asking can seem puzzling at first. As we have learned, the law of attraction is a constant force that is always at work behind the curtain manifesting our desires. Your subconscious mind is the driving force behind this proverbial curtain. You have also learned that what you think about most you attract into your life. Remember, like attracts like, and to quote James Allen's book *As a Man Thinketh*:

"Men do not attract that which they want, but that which they are." Keeping this in mind, we can acknowledge that the mere act of being who we are and the vibrational plane we emulate is a rudimentary way of asking for our desires to manifest in the physical realm.

Asking by being is the essence of the law of attraction, and although this act in and of itself will produce physically manifested results, there are additional, more refined ways of asking that can help manifest more desirable results. You have already practiced one way of asking by writing your desires down on paper.

When it comes to imagining the details of your desires, there are many schools of thought regarding how in-depth your desires should be.

They may be a specific desire:

"I desire a job at Acme Computer Company in San Jose, CA as a software engineer, making $95,000 per year."

Or you can be more general:

"I desire a job as a software engineer for a company that is stable, has advancement opportunities and pays me a salary that is consistent with my qualifications."

You can even open your options up further by just desiring the feeling:

"I desire a job that allows me to utilize my knowledge and talents, that will pay me fairly and where I am happy."

You can choose how detailed your desires will be. Keep in mind, though, that the more detailed your desires, the more precise your manifestations will become.

Keep in mind when developing your desires that you should present them in a desirable or high vibrational manner. Your desires are things that you want, not what you don't want. It is very common to think of things we don't want in our lives – all the undesirable things. If you have those thoughts, simply turn them around into their opposites. For example, if you don't want to keep gaining weight, turn "I don't want to be fat anymore" into "I am now eating healthy and my body weight is perfect."

Another method of inscriptive asking is to convert your desires into "I am" affirmations. I usually combine this method with my gratitude declarations and write something like:

"I am very grateful to be blessed with a number-one bestselling book."

"I am so grateful that I am able to serve others and share knowledge and insight with this book."

"I am thankful for my good health as well as my mental and physical acuity."

"I am grateful for _____."

With pen in hand, my favorite technique that was taught to me by a gentleman named Nelson Berry it is what I call my "I am four-forty journal." Just as the name implies, it's a journal of my desire(s) that I write in daily using a four-step process. This technique requires your daily commitment for up to forty days. Why forty days and not twenty-one, twenty-eight or even thirty days as most other programs advertise? The number forty has a very deep symbolic and divine meaning. Throughout history and throughout most every religion, the number forty has been used to represent a time period of change. Be it forty days or forty years, God always uses forty, and since He created us, He's the one who really knows how long we need – I'm not going to argue with God!

Here is the "I am four-forty" technique. Remember, this is a daily exercise that is best completed before you go to bed, so make it part of your nightly routine.

To begin, start with your journal and write "Day 1" at the top of a blank page.

Step 1: Write down your desire. It could be a physical object, or a situation, and you need to attach an emotion to the desire. Write it in the present tense. I'll use money as an example.

"I am now earning over $6,000 per month. I am so happy and grateful for this income and the opportunities it brings to enhance my life and to be a blessing to others."

Step 2: Show your gratitude and self-support. Gratitude is the most powerful LOA exercise. It raises your vibrational energy and brings you into harmony with the energy of the Universe. Self-support reminds and reassures you that you are deserving of all things wonderful! You are a child of the most high God, and it has been declared time and time again that you are worthy.

"I am grateful for my $6,000 per month income, and I support myself in making this income. I am worthy, and I deserve this wonderful life and this wonderful income."

Step 3: Live "As If." This is where you get to really crank up the imaginative juices. In this step, I want you to write down all of the incredible things that are happening in your life and in the lives of others as a result of this fulfilled desire. Remember to write in the present tense – this reality is actually being created and experienced right now by you in your vibrational reality. The more detailed you get, the better. I want you to really feel the emotions and write them out in detail. Actually begin to live it in your imagination. Remember, everything in our physical reality began in someone's imagination. I always spend at least five minutes on step three every night. It's a very fun thing to do, so have a ball!

"I am so happy now that I make $6,000 per month. My life has really changed! I am much more relaxed and relieved now that I am blessed with more than enough money to joyously pay my monthly bills as well as share this gift of prosperity with many others. Today, I gave a large donation to the children's hospital and blessed a family at the grocery store by buying them popcorn and candy for the kids and renting them a DVD. I was really tickled when the cashier asked me if I knew them, and I told her no. I am looking forward to tomorrow with great excitement and the opportunity to enjoy my life and the opportunity to be a blessing to someone else."

Step 4: Thank your higher source. Much like step two, show your gratitude and thank your divine source for these wonderful blessings. Be sure to state this in the present tense because it is happening right now!

"Thank you, God, for blessing me with this $6,000-per-month income. I am very, very grateful for this gift of abundance and prosperity, as well as the opportunities you give me to share and spread joy. Thank you."

Remember to keep everything in the present tense and really use your imagination every night to experience the feelings and emotions from this fulfilled desire. And most importantly, do this every night for forty nights. If you break the cycle, I recommend you start over. I have learned to discipline myself with this rule, and it really keeps me on track. But most of all, have fun with it!

The third technique of asking is what is known as the "pink bubble," a technique popularized by Shakti Gawain. This is a mental visualization exercise that helps sharpen your mind's eye and creative imagination.

Find a quiet and comfortable place to sit or lie down for this quick five-minute routine. As you will be performing this with your eyes closed, you may be more comfortable in a dark or dimly lit room, or even wear an eye mask.

After you settle in, relax. Imagine what you would like to manifest and think of it as if it has already happened or is happening right now. Actually see yourself in your mind's eye experiencing the scenario. After all, this is your desire and you are the star of the show! Just as you did in the 'I am four-forty journal', see, feel and sense every feeling and emotion you can imagine. Picture it as clearly as you can.

In your mind's eye, place this vision inside a pink bubble. Pink is the color of your heart. It represents your heart's desire.

Then, imagine going to your favorite place in the world (mine is Disneyland) and let go of the bubble. Visualize the bubble floating off into the universe, containing your vision. State to yourself silently or out loud *"I now release this desire into the universe. This, or something better now manifests for me in perfectly satisfying and harmonious ways for the highest good of all concerned."* Watch it as it gets smaller and smaller as it floats up and away. Allow the bubble to float around in the universe, attracting and gathering energy for its manifestation. As soon as the bubble is out of sight, sincerely say "thank you" three times to your higher source and the power of the Universe for manifesting your desire.

Remember, these methods of asking should be focused on one desire at a time. If you send mixed or multiple desires, you will receive mixed and often undesirable results. Remember, we attract into our life, what we think about most, so think about one true desire often and with true emotion and know that you deserve it and that it has already been manifested in your vibrational reality.

I AM
Always
Focused on
the What

Chapter 12

I AM Always Focused on the What

You create the "What" let divine universal power create the "How and "When" for you.

The big three questions are: What do I want? How do I get it? And when do I get it? These questions seem to top most everyone's list when first developing and honing their LOA skills, and with good reason. We have already learned how to find our true desires and we have learned various ways of asking for what we want. It's the next two questions that are on the forefront of everyone's mind once question number one has been answered.

This may sound a bit odd or tricky, but the answer to "How do I get it?" is "It's already done!" Similarly, the answer to "When do I get it?" is "It's already done!" When you were asking for your desire to be fulfilled, you already have manifested it on your vibrational plane; therefore, whatever it is that you are desiring has already been manifested.

Okay, I can hear your "yeah right" BS meter going off again, so let me explain. As we learned earlier, you must release any "need" for your desire and enjoy its vibrational manifestation while it's in your imagination. Once this is accepted in your subconscious, Divine Universal Energy then initiates the process of physical manifestation. How is it done? Well, simply put, that responsibility belongs to the divine universe not you. Your how-to's are very limited, but Divine universal power is not. As stated in the Bible,

"With man this is impossible, but with God all things are possible." Matthew 19:26.

If you look out your window right now, you will most likely see a few trees. Now think of how many trees there are on the entire planet and compare that to how many trees you see out your window. Looking out your window is like looking at your "how" list in comparison to all the trees in the world. That, my friend, is why you don't have to come up with the how. You need only have the faith and belief in your higher source. And as for the when, that is also divine intervention, which requires faith and belief.

Your responsibility is to stay on the high vibrational plane, stay in faith and believe that your desire or something better is now being physically manifested into your reality. How long it will take, from my experience, depends on the situation as well as your vibrational level of consciousness.

At this point, I often see people trying to take on the responsibility for the How and When, only to get frustrated and then come to the conclusion that this LOA stuff is a bunch of bull.

Let's go on a trip from San Francisco to New York. You've been told by many who have gone before you that there is a highway called I-80 that will take you all the way to New York! You've read about it, heard people talk about it, blog about it, and tweet about it, so you say "Let's give it a try and see if this I-80 thing really does work and get us to New York." You jump onto I-80 and begin your trip to New York full of excitement about arriving in New York City! But after three days you make it to Omaha, Nebraska, and haven't seen a single sign mentioning New York. By this time, you get tired of driving and come to the conclusion that this I-80 stuff is a bunch of bull, so you turn around and go back to San Francisco proclaiming that after three whole days of driving, not one sign of New York and that this I-80 thing really doesn't work. See how silly that sounds?

While I was in the Air Force, I was stationed at Nellis AFB in Las Vegas. One day, while waiting for my friend to get off work at a casino, I heard all sorts of commotion. I went over to see what was going on. My friend, who was a cocktail server there, told me that a man had been playing this slot machine for about four or five hours and then just got up and walked away. Right after that, another man went over to the slot machine, sat down, fed it a few silver dollars, pulled the handle and hit the million-dollar jackpot! Now I am not condoning gambling or suggesting you go hit the casino with all your money and all your faith. I share this story as an example of losing faith and giving up when you are just one pull away from hitting the jackpot.

Remember, all you need to do is maintain faith and a high level of vibrational energy. This is easily done by choosing to show and share your happiness, your gifts, your gratitude, and exercise your imagination by living "As If".

I AM Living "As If"

Chapter 13

I AM Living "As If"

Your indestructible faith

By living with the "as if", you stay focused on your desire. Mentally living "as if" helps you to develop and maintain high vibrational energy. There are several techniques available that I have found to be very effective in maintaining your "as if" energy. Here are some that have worked great for myself and many others.

I addition to your "I am four forty" journal, vision boards are a very effective way to subliminally program your subconscious mind. In fact, subliminal marketing is incredibly effective and is used extensively throughout the advertising world. So, why not create your very own ads and market your desires to your inner, subconscious audience. Vision boards are fun to make and fun to use. You can make them out of poster boards, and glue pictures and sayings onto them. You can also create them with your computer. However you choose to make your vision boards, make sure they're visible and looked at often. I always write "I am" affirmations on all of my vision boards. These really help boost my faith and belief, and keep me focused. If I am desiring a material item, such as a car for example, I have many choices of manufacturers, styles and prices. All too often we find something we like and the first thing that pops into our mind is that it's too expensive or out of our price range. Now stop for a second and think what you just affirmed. You just declared a very low vibrational emotion of lack and unworthiness. As like attracts like, you now are in the process of creating or co-creating an environment or reality that will support your lack and unworthiness. Ah, the law of attraction hard at work for you.

On your vision boards, affirm "I am always blessed with more than enough money to purchase anything I truly desire." I learned this little trick from my friend David Hooper. You can adjust and adapt this affirmation for any situation that you desire. I absolutely love what Rhonda Byrne, in her book The Secret, suggests! She says whenever you see something you like, say to yourself "I can afford that _____!"

You can say this whenever you see a car that you like, or a house, a pair of shoes, the biggest latest and greatest whatever. The point here is that you are attaching an emotion to a vision by affirming a desirable statement with the image of your desire. You can add any affirmations to your vision boards that will help you stay focused on the high vibrational plane.

John Assaraf tells a great story about one of his vision boards. As he was moving into his newly purchased and renovated home, he was unpacking some boxes with his young son. In one box was a collection of some of his vision boards from years gone by. His son asked him "What are these, Daddy?" John pulled out some of the old vision boards and started explaining the process to his inquisitive son. While looking at a vision board, he had made more than five years prior, he realized that the house on the vision board was the very same house he had just purchased and was moving into. Back when he created the vision board five years prior, he had no idea where this house was, what it cost or any other details. It was just a picture of a beautiful house he had cut out of a *Dream Homes Magazine*.

There are many stories of people arranging their physical realities in order to accommodate their visionary or vibrational reality. Remember, everything in the physical realm has manifested from someone's vibrational reality. These stories include one of a lady who desired a husband so she arranged her home to be "their" home. She divided the closet space, bathroom space, bought him a recliner, cleared out the garage so there was room for his car, and for over three years, she set two place settings at the dinner table. And yes, it eventually happened, and they have been happily married for over thirty years now.

Living "as if" strengthens your faith and your belief, and keeps making it stronger. Living "as if" allows you to feel and express all of the fantastic and joyous emotions your desire enhances.

The idea of living "as if" is the same as living with expectancy. When you are expecting a baby, you prepare for his or her arrival. You get all the necessary items needed to care for your baby and you excitedly wait for the special day! Before the baby is born, you are living "as if"!

Before you go on vacation, you visualize how fun your adventure will be. In your mind, you are already lying on the beach in Hawaii, or screaming down the Matterhorn at Disney World! This is living "as if!" You see it, feel it, live it and enjoy it, all while it is in your imagination, i.e., your visionary or vibrational reality.

It's the feeling of expectancy, knowing that it is already yours. Just like when you gaze at your presents under the Christmas tree or on the gift table at your birthday party.

Be sure to imagine yourself as having already achieved this desire. See yourself doing the things you'll be doing when it physically manifests, feel and enjoy the emotion. Lock in that feeling and enjoy it every time you think about your desire.

In this chapter, instead of starting with a quote, I leave you with one.

"One cannot be prepared for something while secretly believing it will not happen."

Nelson Mandela

I AM
Affirming
My Desires

Chapter 14

I AM Affirming My Desires

Creating affirmations

*"Every time you read or listen to an affirmation,
it becomes a stronger force in your life."*

– Oprah.

*"By repeating an affirmation over and over again, it becomes
embedded in the subconscious mind, and eventually becomes your
reality."*

– Tony Robbins

Affirmations are, in my opinion, the most effective way to influence your core beliefs and alter your present reality. We are a product of our beliefs and our choices in life. Many of these beliefs were instilled in us when we were young, beliefs that have been passed down through family. These beliefs include, for example, religious practices, health remedies, fears and superstitions and even cooking instructions.

In fact, I once heard a story about a woman who always cuts off the ends of the ham before she puts it in the oven. When asked why she did that, she replied "Because that is how my mother cooked ham." One day her curiosity raised and she asked her own mother the same question. Her mother's answer was the same. "Because that's how my mother cooked ham." With further investigation, it turned out that the woman's great, great grandmother had to cut off the ends of her ham too. However, she had done it because the roasting pan and the oven was too small for an entire ham to fit.

If you are now ready for a change, remember Einstein's definition of insanity as doing the same thing over and over but expecting different results. Having the desire points you in the right direction. Taking that first step is the action necessary for achievement. A desire without self-motivated action is merely a wish with little chance of coming true.

I've shared with you the techniques I've used to re-program the core beliefs that have significantly and desirably changed my life. Now, I would like to share some tips about affirmations.

The intension of an affirmation is to generate a specific emotional feeling spawned by the manifestation of a specific desire. By using our imagination, our words create mental images, which in turn create feelings or emotions. It's the energy of these emotions, or thought vibrations, which broadcast, outward, both mentally and then physically, to manifest our desires into reality.

As the Law of Attraction dictates, your resulting manifestations will match the feelings you get when saying your affirmations.

I always start my affirmations with "I am." I believe there is a divine and miraculous power behind the "I am" that I am, and whatever follows "I am" is therefore blessed with this influence. Starting your affirmations with "I am" also puts them into the present tense. By doing so, you're tapping into your "as if" imagination and generate desirable feelings and emotions such as joy, love, happiness and gratitude. The result will cause a shift in your reality, thus manifesting your desire.

Remember, thoughts create things, so if your thoughts are focused on "I will," then you will enter a never-ending state of "I Will-ness" and your result will be a hopeful feeling for a better future rather than your targeted desired feeling or emotion generated by the manifestation of your desire. Affirming in the present tense ("I am" vs. "I will") also ensures that your subconscious mind immediately goes to work on creating an environment to manifest the desire. There is a great difference between saying "I will be so happy when..." and saying "I am so happy now that...".

Only use words that have desirable and high vibrational energy. Don't use low-energy words like stop, quit, avoid, no longer, or lose. Avoid verbs and phrases that represent lack, such as: I want, I need, or I hope. You should also avoid stating the "problem" within your affirmation. Remember, always affirm what you desire and not what you no longer desire. You can use these low-energy, feelings as indicators of what you do desire. For example, you may feel fat and want to lose weight.

The affirmation,

> "I am no longer going to be fat.
>
> I am losing weight every day,"

may sound desirable, but it is full of nothing but low-energy words and messages for your subconscious to lock into. A more desirable affirmation is: "I am happy to be living a healthy and active lifestyle. I am now only eating healthy foods. I am proud of my beautifully proportioned, fit and trim body."

Remember that your affirmations are only for and about you. Attempting to affirm a change in someone else is what I consider an attempted spell. You have no authority or right to try to cause change in anyone but yourself. Even with your best intentions, what you consider good or right for another person may not be what they desire. The only person you have authority over is yourself. Please know and respect others and their beliefs.

Keep your affirmations as brief as possible. Your subconscious mind does not think in the same terms as your conscious mind. The subconscious thinks in mental pictures. So, using short, precise affirmations give your subconscious mind the information and time it needs to convert the affirmation into a mental image.

The last thing I'd like to suggest about affirmations is that you recite them multiple times per day. For whatever it is that I am actively desiring to manifest into my physical reality, I always create twelve precise and well defined affirmations. I write them down, print them out, make them the background on my computer, iPad and iPhone, hang printed versions throughout my home, make a wallet-sized version to carry with me, record them audibly into my iPod, and read them, look at them, and listen to them over and over and over twenty-four hours per day.

You could say I have a very high level of commitment!

You may also find it as no surprise that I have a very high attractor factor!

I AM Happy, Healthy and Wealthy

A list of effective affirmations for you

I am happy, healthy and wealthy
I am worthy of a great and wonderful life
I am positive in all situations
I am thankful for all of my blessings
I am beautiful inside and out
I am confident and self-assured at all times
I am compassionate and understanding
I am forgiven and forgiving
I am living a peaceful and joyous life
I am blessed with good things happening every day
I am attracting people who reflect my highest good
I am safe, protected, and loved
I am divinely blessed every day in all that I do
I am divinely guided every day in all that I do
I am free to be me
I am completely in acceptance of who I am
I am joyful, enthusiastic and motivated
I am happy and allowing myself to have fun
I am happy with myself and my life
I am a good person who deserves to be happy
I am a co-creator of my reality
I am naturally outgoing and friendly
I am always sharing my smile
I am always calm in all situations
I am at peace with my past
I am in control of my thoughts and emotions
I am full of positive, loving energy
I am grateful for my life
I am always sharing my joy and happiness
I am fit, healthy and attractive
I am thankful for my healing abilities
I am accepting health into my body now

I am grateful for my perfect health
I am enjoying eating healthy and nutritious foods
I am always maintaining my ideal body weight
I am happy living a healthy lifestyle
I am disciplined with my eating habits
I am thankful for my beautiful body
I am a healthy eater
I am in excellent health
I am physically fit
I am my ideal weight
I am grateful for my perfect health
I am naturally healthy and strong
I am divinely guided with perfect health
I am in peak physical condition
I am proud of my beautiful, healthy, strong body
I am healed
I am grateful for my abundance and prosperity
I am attracting financial wealth every day
I am worthy of financial abundance
I am happy to share my financial wealth
I am creating blessings for others with my prosperity
I am attracting the energy of abundance all the time
I am always focused on attracting prosperity
I am divinely blessed with financial abundance
I am a successful money manager
I am receiving a great income doing what I love
I am confident in my ability to attract and create wealth
I am always motivated and get things done
I am abundance and prosperity
I am a financial blessing to many people
I am a divine instrument of abundance and prosperity
I am grateful that I can help others financially
I am deserving and worthy of financial abundance
I am grateful for my wealth and abundance
I am always helping others
I am now enjoying great financial abundance

I am always blessed with financial security
I am divinely loved and cared for
I am happy, healthy and wealthy

MESSAGE FROM AUTHOR R. J. BANKS

I gladly share my knowledge and advice, at first just one on one, but then I began publicly posting the question and my insight on the Facebook page. Soon I was very busy sharing my knowledge and feeling very much like the Dear Abby of the Law of Attraction. It was during this time that I was encouraged and inspired to write

"The Power of I AM and the Law of Attraction."

I am a lover of wisdom (aka a "Philosopher") and a passionate student of life who is committed to inspiring and empowering millions of people to live their greatest lives. As I study, embody and share my knowledge and interpretation of inspired optimal living and co-creating a life we all deserve as God's children, I have found that true joy and happiness is in serving and helping others.

We are, and attract into our lives, what we think, say and believe about ourselves and our perceived reality.

R. J. BANKS

R.J. Banks is an active speaker, radio talk show host, radio personality, coach and author.

You can find more on R.J. Banks at these Resources

www.loaaffirmations.com Audio Affirmation programs

www.facebook.com/loaaffirmations Active Facebook Page

www.loaradionetwork.com and loaradionetwork.com/rj-banks.html Weekly radio show broadcast
"The Power of the I AM"

www.loaevent.com and www.loaevent.com/rj-banks April 2014 LOA Radio Event

http://about.me/rjbanks About Me page

www.robbanksvoiceovers.com Voice-over business website

For more books published by

Crystal City Publishing

Visit us at:

www.CrystalCityPublishing.com